How
People
Like a Book

What Everyone Should Know About
Body Language, Emotions and NLP to
Decode Intentions, Connect Effortlessly,
and Develop Effective Communication
Skills

Richard Hawkins

express written consent from the publisher. All additional rights reserved.

The information in the following pages is broadly considered to be a truthful and accurate account of facts and as such any inattention, use or misuse of the information in question by the reader will render any resulting actions solely under their purview. There are no scenarios in which the publisher or the original author of this work can be in any fashion deemed liable for any hardship or damages that may befall them after undertaking information described herein.

Additionally, the information in the following pages is intended only for informational purposes and should thus be thought of as universal. As befitting its nature, it is presented without assurance regarding its prolonged validity or interim quality. Trademarks that are mentioned are done without written consent and can in no way be considered an endorsement from the trademark holder.

Table of Contents

Introduction...7

Chapter 1: How to Read People Mastering Communication in a Business Environment 11

Chapter 2: How to Read People Mastering Communication in a Learning Environment 31

Chapter 3: How to Read People Mastering Interpersonal Communication................. 47

Chapter 4: How to Read People Mastering Advertorial Communication.................... 72

Chapter 5: How to Read People Mastering Active Listening 86

Chapter 6: How to Read People Mastering Nonverbal Communication 96

Conclusion 113

Introduction

Congratulations on downloading this book and thank you for doing so.

The following chapters will discuss the information you need to master the most advanced elements of communication. It breaks down the different types of communication that you will engage in on a regular basis.

You will start your journey about learning how to master communication in a business environment. This can help you to better communicate with colleagues at all levels as well as with any other person you would encounter at work.

The next step is exploring communication in learning. Being a lifelong learner is needed for success in all areas of life. You will then delve into communicating best with those in your personal life. Both of these areas ensure that you are getting more out of the world around you and your personal relationships.

Knowing more about how marketing and advertising impact your daily life is important. When you master this form of communication, it makes it easier to ensure that you are making the best purchasing and financial decisions.

Listening is half of the battle when it comes to being an effective communicator. You want to ensure that you can actively listen and properly interpret what other people are trying to tell you. This ensures that you can respond in the best way possible.

The last step is making sure that you master nonverbal communication. This includes your own as well as being able to read it in other people.

There are plenty of books on this subject on the market; thanks again for choosing this one! Every effort was made to ensure it is full of as much useful information as possible, please enjoy!

Chapter 1: How to Read People Mastering Communication in a Business Environment

Mark Cuban is a multi-millionaire that is known for being self-made. He says that being an effective salesman is the secret to his success. Of course, the foundation of sales success is communication. He said that by working in sales, he learned more about communication than he did anywhere else.

If you have seen him on Shark Tank, you know that a lot of the bets he takes are on unconventional ideas. So, what sets these ideas from the rest that are presented to him? According to him, the people making these seemingly unconventional pitches know how to communicate.

Cuban is known for being incredibly honest and direct. If he has something on his mind, he does not hesitate to make it known to the world. However, he also seems to convey his thoughts in a way that are professional while still being powerful. To sum it up, when he talks, people listen.

Cuban also states that to be a leader, you must be a stellar communicator. This is certainly something that you can see to be true if you look at some of the most famous leaders in history. There are several communication strategies that have been used by history's most famous communicators – from Cuban to Abraham

Lincoln. 10 secrets that you need to know include:

- **Keep it real:** If people do not trust you, no matter what you say, they are not going to believe it fully. Of course, you cannot just demand trust either. You have to let the fact that you are trustworthy shine through your actions, the decisions you make, and what you say and think. Remember that once you lose trust, it is almost impossible to put it back. Put integrity above all else and no matter who you talk to, they will trust what you say.

- **Get personal:** If you are not approachable, what you say will not be heard. Your colleagues and those working below you need to know that you value their thoughts as much as they value theirs. Develop meaningful relationships with those you work with and your communication will be heard in the right way.

- **Be specific:** When you want to send out a message, be clear and concise; clarity and brevity are underappreciated in today's world. Get the main point across right away and ditch the fluff. This ensures that all of your words count.

- **Focus on what is left behind:** It is common to put most of your focus on the takeaways when you are delivering information. However, you want to put just as much emphasis on what you leave behind. This means that you have to consider how people take the overall contribution of your message as well as what the recipients of your communication want. When you attend to the recipient's desires, you are making sure that you are conveying your message in a way that they will best hear it and learn from it.

- **Open your mind:** This should go without saying, but it can be difficult to put your biases aside especially if you are the person in charge. When your mind is open, this is something that people will notice. Do not make your dissenting opinions the focus of any communication. Make sure that those you communicate with know that you are willing to hear their side and learn just as you expect them to do. Think of this as a reciprocal idea exchange.

- **Listen as much as you talk:** Half of effective communication is listening. This means not only hearing another person's words but actually understanding their stance and why they are saying what they are saying. No communication should ever be one-sided or closed. When you present an idea, make it clear that you want those on the receiving end to provide their thoughts and actually listen when they provide them.

- **Use empathy over ego:** Ego has its place in business, but you need to know when to toss it aside and let empathy take the reins. Your empathy needs to be conveyed in a way that is transparent and authentic. Basically, when you are empathetic, it has to be because you truly are, or people will see right through it. When you show empathy at the right times, you will earn respect, and when people respect you, everything that you communicate is received as you intend it to be.

- **Read between the lines:** You have likely heard this saying before; all master communicators can read between the lines. Eliminate the rhetoric and quickly cut through the primary ideas to find the underlying message. Then, when you convey thoughts and ideas, make sure that your underlying message shines through as much as your primary one.

- **Know your topic:** You will explore this element of communication more in chapter two, but it is worth mentioning here, too. Do not speak with authority on topics you are not an expert on. Or else, you will quickly lose the interest of those listening to you. However, when you do have command over a topic, let your verbal and nonverbal communication show this.

- **Make groups feel like individuals:** At work, it is common to speak to multiple people at once to increase workplace efficiency. However, each member of the group should feel like you are talking to them directly.

In addition to the 10 facts above, you also need to know when it is time to either change your message or the way that you are delivering it. When you are speaking to a person or group, pay attention to how they are receiving your words. Do they seem to be engaged and really hearing you, or do they seem distant and uninterested? If the latter, you might want to switch up your delivery method. Find a way to shorten what you have to say or make it clearer. Add in humor, analogies, questions, stories, or relevant data that are appropriate to make it more interesting.

If you are trying to deliver a message and it is just not landing right, adjust your message. Think of ways to deliver the same details, but in a way that is different and more engaging. For example, if your message is that you need to increase sales by 20 percent, simply telling people this might feel a bit forced or like they are being lectured. Instead, deliver this in a way that is upbeat and make sure that they know that it will be a team effort. Ask for their input and make them feel as though they are part of the process as more than just a worker bee. You are still saying you need to increase sales by

20 percent, but with the right adjustment, they will hear you better and grasp the sense of urgency you are trying to communicate.

Oprah is another businesswoman that is completely self-made. As one of the world's most successful people, she credits her rise to the top to her communication skills. She says that the most important element of communication is the ability to connect with those you are communicating with. She said that what is more important is what makes people alike instead of what makes them different. When you find a place where you connect with your audience, you will have their undivided attention. You will connect with something that you have in common.

Oprah says that people need to know that you value them. Their value to you has to be clear in all communications that you have with them. Ask them what they want. Ask them their thoughts and opinions. When they are speaking, really listen to them. When a person feels valued by you, everything that you say will come across loud and clear. It also ensures that you get the valuable information that you need.

Oprah says communication is very similar to a dance. One person steps forward and the other steps back. A single misstep can lead both parties on the floor – tangled together and confused. She says that when this happens, you need to stop and just listen. Ask for clarification if you need it. This starts getting into active listening which you will learn more about in another chapter. Basically, with this element of communication, you are telling the other person, "I hear you."

There are five different communication skills that are imperative in the business world. Once you master these, there is no situation that you will not be able to handle. These are skills that you need – starting with your first interview and going through to your retirement.

Watch the body language of your recipient when you are communicating. In a future chapter, you will get the details about body language and nonverbal communication but introducing it here is important. By paying attention to what someone is saying without their words makes it easier to know if your message is being delivered successfully. You also need to ensure that your words and body language are not in conflict with one another.

Technology is a major component of business today. It is used for all elements of work, and this includes workplace communication. You will use technology, such as slideshows and videos, when you are giving presentations and delivering other forms of communication. When you are creating a video or slideshow, it must back up your message. However, it also cannot interfere with or outshine it. This is a balance that you have to learn how to strike. The overall quality of your technology communication aids must also be superior.

No matter how big or small your audience is, you have to be able to listen as you speak. Of course, you will want to hear questions and ensure that you can respond in a meaningful way. However, you also have to listen to the subtler sounds of your audience. Are people yawning or sighing when you talk? This generally indicates boredom and when people are bored, they are not really hearing what you have to say.

Your verbal communication must be crystal clear at all times. There is a saying that says to never use $1,000 words when you can use a $10 word. This means that you want to keep your language simple. Avoid jargon and be very straightforward. Even if you are talking to people with a specific expertise, it is still better to keep it simple. Keep your opinions out of it and know that your ultimate goal is to get the key points delivered with clarity. Earlier in this chapter, you learned that brevity and clarity are paramount. This is true and should be your goal when verbally communicating.

As part of any business, at least a portion of your communication will be written. You need to be able to deliver any message written that you could verbally. Working on improving your writing skills is imperative. Whether you are writing a report, a proposal, or even a memo, superior writing skills are needed. When you write well, not only it is professional, but it ensures that your words are understood as you intend them.

Now that you know more about these five skills, think about the business people you know who expertly execute them; Steve Jobs is a good example. He used an array of communication techniques when giving presentations. He also always paid attention to how the audience reacted to what he had to say. This allowed him to quickly pivot and adjust his delivery if he started to lose the attention of his audience.

When Jobs spoke, he did so with passion and conviction. He truly believed in his ideas and he gave credit where it was due. He provided demonstrations, told stories, and used a language that made it possible for every person in the audience to understand what he was saying. He never muddled his message and he focused on a single idea at a time. He used videos and slideshows to further his points and to provide additional clarification.

Many of Jobs' colleagues said that when he spoke to an audience, they felt like they were the only person in the room. He moved freely but was an expert at providing individual attention even in the largest of auditoriums. Forbes has said many times that Jobs was the ultimate communicator. This is because his style was complex, but it had a simplicity that allowed every person listening to learn.

This is certainly a lot of information to process. Start with one bit at a time. Take note of your current communication style and think about how your colleagues tend to receive the information that you provide. This will help you to see which areas require the most work so that you can formulate a plan which will allow you to effectively improve your business communication.

To sum it up, consider the following when executing communication in the workplace:

- Consider open meetings
- Treat emails and major presentations the same
- Consider one-on-one for important information
- Consider training sessions for communication skills for your entire workplace
- Take advantage of technology presentations

- Be confident, but know when to utilize empathy
- Use visual aids
- Keep your words simple
- Mind your body language and pay attention to the nonverbal communication of your audience
- Listen to those you are talking to
- Act out your message
- Avoid unnecessary repetition
- Use the right voice tone
- Create a receptive atmosphere
- Be articulate
- Never mumble
- Incorporate humor where appropriate
- Gesticulate
- Encourage feedback
- Be appreciative

Chapter 2: How to Read People Mastering Communication in a Learning Environment

Learning and teaching is something that you do on a daily basis. In some cases, it is almost an unconscious process. To learn, or to teach, proper and effective communication is critical. Looking at some of the most effective teachers and some of the most knowledgeable people is a solid way to see how it is done. You also want to learn the intricate details concerning communication with teaching and learning so that you can adopt the most successful techniques.

You as the Learner

Every day you will find new opportunities to learn. For example, your employer wants to use a software program. You will need to learn this. You might also learn how to navigate to a new destination, how to troubleshoot a problem with an appliance, or how to get along with a new neighbor. Learning is constant.

When you are trying to learn something new, communication is at the foundation of this. You have to be able to listen effectively, ask clear questions, and convey any confusion that you might have. As a learner, there are five communication skills you must master to get the most out of every learning experience.

The first is verbal communication. You have to be able to convey your weaknesses and ask questions to get clarification. In a classroom, you will give presentations and work on group projects – both of which require you to be able to communicate clearly and effectively.

Secondly, you need strong listening skills. No matter the medium you are using for learning, you have to be able to hear and understand what your teacher is telling you. This is true whether you are in a lecture class or if you are reading a manual to learn how to change your car's oil. You have to be able to pick out the most important information and know how to connect different lessons to see the big picture.

Writing and learning go hand in hand. You have to be able to demonstrate your understanding of an idea by writing it out. You will do this in school and at work. In fact, writing daily is one of the most effective ways to learn.

Interpersonal communication skills are critical in a learning environment. You often cannot choose who you learn from, so you have to be able to effectively communicate with teachers from all walks of life.

Body language is also critical. You have to be able to make your body language match your message as well as decode body language.

The good news is that you can learn to develop your learner-based communication skills. Start by making it a habit to analyze eye contact and body language. From here, work on summarizing, responding, and paraphrasing the key points of the lessons that you are working on. The following methods are ways to help work on building your communication skills for the purpose of becoming an effective learner:

- Watch films and television and analyze the communication elements of the characters

- Work on your active listening skills

- Take advantage of technology – especially items and elements that are focused on enhancing your ability to communicate or those that make communication easier

- When you ask questions, make sure that they are open-ended since these invite further learning opportunities

- When in a classroom environment, take advantage of all oral presentations and group assignments

- Work on your critical thinking skills. A major element of communication is being able to think critically before delivering your communication

- Look for opportunities to teach others. When you can put yourself in a teacher's shoes, it makes it easier to be receptive to their lessons

- Record lessons, take notes, and at the end of the day, use these to reflect on what you learned. This is also a chance to better hone your active listening skills

As with all things, you want to take every opportunity you can to enhance your communication skills, too. There are some exercises that you can do regularly to build your communication skills and assess your progress.

You have learned that body language and nonverbal communication are critical. Write a short speech and recite it while looking in the mirror. Make sure that this is a full-length mirror because you want to see your entire body. Look at your posture and pay attention to your facial expressions.

Record yourself with this same speech and then listen to it. Were you clear and concise? Was your tone neutral? Were you speaking with authority? Evaluate the overall speech and see which areas you need to work on.

Write often and then look back at your writing. Just like your verbal communication, it should be clear, easy to read, and quickly get to the point. You also want to look at the overall mechanics of your writing. Ensure that there are no typos, grammatical errors or punctuation mistakes.

You as the Teacher

Whether you are a teacher, you are training a new coworker, or you are helping your child with their homework, excellent communication skills are needed to ensure that you are effective. In fact, it is said that teaching is half knowledge and half effective communication. Simply providing someone with information is not enough. You need to deliver this information in a way that makes it possible for them to truly absorb it.

When you are teaching, you do not necessarily need to be an accomplished expert in the subject matter. You simply need to make the person you are teaching feel confident in your abilities – this is all communication. You also need to be able to communicate effective and creative solutions to problems that your students might face.

The first step is talking to whom you are teaching. You have to get to know them, their learning style, and what their weaknesses and strengths are. Remember that trust and feeling valued are important for being able to trust the person talking to you. Your students must know that you care and that you are worth their attention.

Once you get over this communication hurdle, the next thing to do is to take inventory of the student's strengths and weaknesses. Ask them what they think they are. This gives you a starting point. From here, you can craft lessons and evaluate their performance for more detailed information.

Lastly, you need to know how to communicate to best reach the student's specific learning style. There are seven learning styles to learn how to effectively communicate with:

- **Visual:** This learner does best with images, pictures, and spatial understanding. You will need to utilize these to communicate your lesson. For example, instead of just telling your child the steps required to tie their shoes, you would create photos of each of the steps. By looking at these as they go along, they can visualize the process, making it easier for them to interpret and memorize.

- **Verbal:** Words are the best way to teach this learning and this includes both writing and speech. You must communicate your words clearly and get straight to the point. Use real-life examples to better bring the lessons to life. Pay attention to their body language because this will tell you if they are truly hearing what you have to say.

- **Logical:** This learner requires reasoning, logic, and systems to learn best. You will need to make sure that all of your communications avoid hypothetical situations. Keep it basic and any props or aids should be concise and avoid too much creativity.

- **Solitary:** This type of learner does best with self-study. This is where your written communication skills will come into play. You will need to create lessons or directions completely in written form. For the most part, you will just use words and you do not have to worry about photos and visual aids.

- **Aural:** Music and sound work well for this type of learner. You can create songs together to help with tasks, such as memorization. You might also consider recording your verbal lessons for the person to listen to when they are ready to learn.

- **Physical:** The sense of touch and physical movement is important for this learner. You will also need to be mindful of your body language when teaching a physical learner. They can more easily pick up on nonverbal cues, and if yours are negative or guarding, it can negatively impact their learning experience.

- **Social:** If you have a social learner, they do best in groups. When you are working with a group, you must evenly divide your communication and attention among the people in the group.

John Locke is an example of a teacher who changed the way the world looks at learning. He made clear the value of academics but said that a person's character development is even more important. To help develop a student's character requires effective communication. You need to know how to reach them on a deep level. You also need to know how to communicate with them in a way that makes them think. You have to be able to challenge them in a way that is exciting and engaging without negative pressure.

Another example is Kazuya Takahashi. This Japanese teacher uses creative competition and LEGO-based instruction. He not only teaches his students the basic skills needed to graduate but also how to use communication to find their own independence. He combines communication skills with creativity to boost their confidence and help them to see that their individuality is an asset.

No matter their learning style, the following communication skills for teachers are ones that you want to work on mastering:

- Listen
- Give praise
- Describe clear goals
- Use humor
- Be accessible
- Embrace variety
- Build teamwork
- Keep it real

Chapter 3: How to Read People Mastering Interpersonal Communication

Interpersonal communication is how you essentially interact with the people in your life, as well as the strangers that you run into on a daily basis. It is important that you know how to properly communicate with all people. There are a number of advanced techniques that you can work on which will make your communication skills stronger. As you work on these, you will notice positive changes in all of your relationships.

Communicating with Family Members

Families are always an interesting dynamic. For the most part, the communication skills needed to connect with them are mostly basic. Families already have a connection even if certain relationships are strained. This helps to dictate the best methods for ensuring effective and neutral conversation. Consider the following to make sure that conversations with family members have the intended result:

- Create opportunities to have conversations with people in your family and do not be afraid to engage in tough conversations when they are warranted

- Find time to have gatherings with family members that are built around catching up with each other

- Utilize the 80/20 rule when you are engaging in conversation. This means that you want to listen 80 percent of the time and talk 20 percent of the time. This ensures that every person involved in the conversation has the chance to contribute in a meaningful way

- Do not restrict conversations to only adults unless having children present would be inappropriate. When you involve family members of all ages this not only allows you to work on this type of interpersonal communication, but it opens you up to new ideas and information

- Know when to agree to disagree. This is important. Just because you are family, it does not mean that you are all going to agree on everything. Use active listening to truly hear other perspectives and agree to disagree to those you cannot get onboard with

Communicating with Strangers

Even though your interactions with strangers are generally brief, you want to make sure that any communication is positive and pleasant. There is a saying that states that you meet every person for a reason. A person you have a five-minute conversation with has the ability to have a lasting impact on your life when the communication is proper and clear. There have been stories on the news where a person says that they were considering suicide until a stranger took a minute to notice them and have a brief conversation. This shows you how powerful effective communication can be.

There are some advanced communication skills that you can employ to make these short exchanges with strangers as meaningful as possible. These include:

- Use your skills for empathic reflection
- Make sure that you are paying attention to nonverbal cues

- Never assume what a person is thinking, their beliefs, or that they will agree with you
- Make sure that you never make snap judgments. Remember the saying that a book's cover is not enough to make a fair judgment
- Stay current on the news but try to stick to more positive events. This will always give you something fun to talk about
- After an interaction with a stranger, think of one thing that you learned. Use the earlier chapter on communication for learners to ensure you can get a lesson from every conversation
- Never overshare with strangers. Keep it simple and positive

- Know when it is time to listen

Communicating with Kids

Communicating with children is a special type of skill. Kids think and act differently than adults do. For the most part, kids need reassurance that you are listening and that you are not thinking less of what they are saying just because they are kids. The first step in this is making sure that you listen actively. Ask questions and let them know that you are interested in what they are saying and that you are enjoying the conversation.

Next, make sure that you are always available. This is especially important as kids get into their teen years because it is common for them to retreat from talking to their parents.

Lastly, make sure that you respond appropriately. If you automatically show anger when you are talking to your child about an issue, this will eventually make them afraid to come to you when they need advice or help. Always be firm but be mindful of their feelings. Make sure to be clear that any reprimanding is because you want to help them to learn. Reassure them that you love them after a tough conversation. This is especially important when it comes to younger children.

Communicating with Romantic Partners

A romantic relationship is a wonderful thing, and strong and effective communication is the foundation. When both of you are skilled communicators, it makes it easier to keep conflict to a minimum. It also ensures that both of you truly know each other. This can be one of the most complex relationships and because of this, there is a lot of information to know to ensure that you are communicating effectively. Remember the following whenever you are communicating:

- Utilize feedback and active listening

- Always be gentle

- Before seeking to be understood, seek to understand

- Edit your criticism

- Stay calm

- Keep your questions open-ended

- Calm yourself before engaging in a conversation about a negative situation

- Put yourself in your partner's shoes

- Always speak up about something that you appreciate and value about your partner

- Use humor during argument situations as it is appropriate

- When you are disagreeing about something, apologize and then validate

- If possible, try to change the subject when the current subject is causing tension

- Make physical contact

- Before tackling an intense conversation, give each other some space

- Always acknowledge your common ground

- Be aware of your body language and that of your partner

- Do not use conversation fillers that are not necessary or pertinent to the conversation

- Plan what you will say if you are discussing something the two of you disagree on.

Communicating with Friends

Friends sometimes have disagreements, and this is okay. Friendships also evolve. When such situations happen, it is important that you utilize the proper communication techniques. Be open and honest, but also be receptive to hear what your friend has to say. The following are advice to ensure that your communications with your friends go smoothly and help you overcome any obstacles in your relationships:

- When you tell them how you feel, express this clearly and do not let your emotions become the emphasis

- Use statements with "I," and never be accusatory

- If you do not understand something, ask them to clarify

- Do not wait to address a problem. Get to communicating about it right away

- If raising an issue makes you uncomfortable, make this clear from the beginning

- Pay attention to your body language so that it fits the situation that you are talking about

- Make sure that you communicate more about positive feelings than negative ones

The Basic Rules of Interpersonal Communication

You have surely heard of Dr. Phil. He is a television doctor that works to help people improve their communication skills to solve problems and improve relationships. He has six rules for effective interpersonal communication:

- **Insist on emotional integrity:** Be straightforward about what you are feeling or thinking. Do not beat around the bush. If you are angry, use your words to calmly tell the person exactly why you feel this way. Do not just expect someone to be able to just know how you are feeling and why. When you are open and honest, you are not only ensuring better communication, but this will also ultimately lead to a stronger relationship over time. No matter how hard the subject is to discuss, it is important that you are not afraid to do it.

- **Be a two-way communicator:** Remember that it takes at least two people to be able to communicate. You cannot just be a listener or a talker. When you read about relationship issues, it is common for one partner to say that the other just never listen. You must be in tune with the other person to remain aware of each other's needs and feelings. Relationships are give-and-take, and this has to be within good balance. Make sure to ask questions and give feedback. Of course, you also must be able to handle feedback and answer the questions that are asked of you.

- **Establish a motive:** What do you expect to get out of communication? You need to have both a clear message and a clear motive with anything that you are talking about. The motive is not always clear. Sometimes it takes another person challenging you to be able to uncover what these are. You might have to take a hard look at yourself and confront your own insecurities to determine what your motives are and what your message needs to be.

- **Check in with each other:** Test the messages that the two of you share. Make sure that when you are responding, you are doing so honestly. Do not just try and guess what the other person is trying to say. If you are unsure, ask for clarification. You also need to be honest about your feelings. If someone asks if you are okay and you are not, say this.

- **Be an active listener:** In a later chapter, you will get a chance to delve into the details of active listening. Your ability to listen must be just as strong as your ability to talk. When you can listen well, you will hear everything that the person is saying. You will also be able to better determine if what the person is saying is honest because you will be examining their nonverbal cues as they speak.

- **Evaluate your filters:** When you are communicating with someone, you can only control yourself and your communication techniques. You cannot try and control what they are saying and when they are talking. Make sure to open your mind and do not just dismiss, or "filter out," what you do not want to hear. This is important and something you will have to work on because everyone has their own beliefs about things. Try not to judge and work to be receptive to different ideas and perspectives.

Conflict Resolution for Interpersonal Relationships

No matter your relationship and how close you might be to a person, a conflict will arise on occasion. What is important is how you respond to this conflict. It is important that you do it in a way that does not disrupt the connection that you might have with the person. Conflict resolution is all about communication. There are multiple communication skills, as well as personality skills, that you can strengthen to ensure that you become effective at keeping conflict under control.

- Accept that conflict does happen, and it can even be beneficial as long as you use the right communication techniques to solve it

- During the resolution conversation, make sure to engage in active listening

- Do what you can to keep yourself and all participants in the conversation calm and on topic

- Make sure that your communication is neutral at all times

- Work together to find a solution that all participants can agree on

- Take the time to analyze the conflict before you all start to discuss ways to solve it

- Separate the problem from the person you view as being the initiator

- Do not have a single resolution goal in mind, but try and let the conversation guide you

- Get creative if you need to so that all people involved in the conflict are satisfied by the outcome

- Make sure that you keep your focus on the future

- When you are talking to those involved in the conflict, make sure that every person has a chance to share their feelings and interests

- Depending on the situation and the environment where the conflict takes place, if there is need for confidentiality, ensure that it is maintained at all times

- Be very specific when you are identifying the problem

General Tips for All Interpersonal Communication

There are certain tips that are going to be relevant no matter your relationship with the person. Keep these in mind with every person you are working to communicate with:

- Try to not show your negative body language

- Before you speak, take a second to think about what you are going to say and how you are going to say it
- When another person is talking, give them your full attention and do not interrupt them
- Always be neutral and avoid attacking the other person or getting defensive
- Always utilize active listening
- Never deviate from the topic at hand
- Keep an open mind, especially when you are receiving feedback
- When it comes to your ideas, be confident in them

- Know the different types of communication and use the appropriate one at the appropriate time

- When you shake hands with someone, do so firmly

With this information, you can better ensure that you can communicate with all of the people in your life and around you. Make sure that you are constantly looking for ways to improve your interpersonal communication because it should evolve as you get older and as your relationships either change or grow stronger.

Chapter 4: How to Read People Mastering Advertorial Communication

Advertorial communication is a skill that all people should have. It is the hallmark of marketing and advertising, but all people can use it to ensure that their points are being made clear. There are times in life when you need to persuade people to see things your way. For example, when you go for a job interview, you need to persuade the interviewer that you are the best candidate.

This is where advertorial communication comes into play. By examining persuasive advertising, you can master this communication skill.

Use scare tactics in conversation. This might sound harsh, but it is not. It is basically you who are creating a situation where the person you are communicating with develops a fear of missing out. Now, this must be done with balance because you do not want to lean to the manipulative end of the spectrum. The purpose here is not to manipulate but to make it clear that you are the best person for the job.

Start by introducing your skills and how you developed them. Be quick and clear about this. Next, list the related accomplishments.

For example, if you are a nurse seeking a promotion, what have you done that the other nurses in your unit have not? This is what is going to set you apart and make you a more desirable as a candidate.

Take a look at advertisements for limited edition items for a good example of this. They hype up the products and induce fear to persuade you to make a purchase as soon as possible. This is essentially what you are doing with this communication technique.

Promise happiness in your communication. You have to convince them that by choosing you, they will make the environment happier and more positive. This also happens to be a very basic advertorial technique. You can follow up using scare tactics with this. You essentially induce a healthy level of fear and then bring them back to a happy and positive place. This essentially communicates a level of safety, and they will remember that you provided this sense of safety.

Attack their level of accomplishment in a controlled way. People are worried about how they are perceived. Finding a vulnerability and then building it up makes you memorable. This is another common advertorial technique. For example, you see a car commercial on television. It basically tells you that driving that vehicle will make people respect you and view you as successful. What can you provide that will make the company you are applying to appear more successful and respected? This is what you need to communicate.

Make it clear that you are one of a kind. This is actually harder than it sounds because you have to go outside the norm. Telling them about your discipline, responsible behavior and your education is great and should be said. However, what makes you different from the other candidates that will sit in that same chair for an interview? This is where you have to be unafraid to take a risk. Can you do something uncommon, such as hula hoop for a long period of time? Communicate this. As long as it is an appropriate skill, you might also consider a visual aid since this will stick in the mind of the interviewer. For example, show a short video clip of your hula hooping skills.

Approach the situation with a promise of friendship. Friends are loyal, supportive, and there to catch you when bad things happen. These also happen to be positive traits of employees. Find a way to show the interviewer that you are more than just someone who will clock in, work, and go home. Show them the value of your friendship.

When you are describing your skills and accomplishments, create positive associations. This is something you often see in advertorial campaigns. The brand will have a loved celebrity, for example, endorse their products. Now, you do not want to bring a famous person to the interview with you. Instead, find something fun and positive to associate your accomplishments with. The association should be something the interviewer knows well. This is where you need to do your homework and get to know the company and interviewer. This ensures that the association that you communicate will be received in a positive way. This is another area where a quick and appropriate visual aid can be beneficial.

Make them laugh. Laughter causes the release of brain chemicals that make a person feel good. As you are communicating with the interviewer, you have to know how to time a joke properly. You also need to be able to read their body language and personality to determine if a joke will even go over well. There will always be times when you will meet someone that will not view joking as a good thing, so keep this in mind. This is where your decoding of nonverbal cues and your ability to actively listen will come into play.

Humanize the harsh realities of the industry. No matter what industry you are trying to get into, there are negative elements. Do not be afraid to tackle these and present solutions. Just make sure that you communicate your proposed solutions in a neutral way and bring a human or real-world element to your solutions. This makes them much easier to relate to and envision. This also gives you a chance to create an emotional connection with the interviewer. People like to see the human side of others. It can create a type of instant bond that makes them want to be around you and hire you, eventually.

Utilize imagery when it is appropriate. This is a communication technique that will take some practice. This is a skill that is referred to as visual communication. When you provide visual imagery at the right points during your conversation, it makes it easier for the person you are talking to better connect to what you are saying. The speech, "I Have a Dream" by Dr. Martin Luther King is a fantastic example of flawlessly incorporating imagery into verbal communication. At one point in the speech, he talks about the riches of freedom. He uses terms such as "insufficient funds" and "bad check" to describe how the nation was letting down African American people by denying them a number of basic freedoms. When you listen to the speech, you can imagine seeing the "insufficient funds" phrase blinking on an ATM. Not only does this create rich imagery, but it also creates the perfect opportunity for communicating associations and real-world realities.

Now that you know about the different advertorial communication techniques and how to apply them to different areas of your life, it is time to learn about a more direct approach. The following will be successful whether you are looking to sell yourself via written or verbal communication:

- Know who you are and make sure that you can convey this clearly. You cannot beat around the bush when you are telling someone why you are the best. You have to speak with purpose and authority. You also want to speak or write with passion, but do not let this get away from you. You have to still embrace brevity.

- Do not be afraid to tell a story when you are working to describe yourself and your merits. You are essentially telling your story, so do it in a way that is informative but also interesting. Be articulate and do not be afraid to drop in powerful statements that are appropriate. Most of all, make sure that you are authentic and honest.

- Know the person you are talking to. For example, if you are going for a job interview, take the time to research the company and the person who will be conducting the interview. You want to know the culture of the company and the overall personality of the interviewer. This makes it easier to tailor the delivery method of your communication. For example, if the company you are applying to has an open and youthful culture, you would not go into the interview wearing expensive and fancy clothing and being too buckled up. You would want to ensure that you come off as fun and this would be an appropriate situation to inject creativity and humor.

- Know where you will best match, and do not be shy about denying opportunities you do not match up with. There is no shame in saying "no" if you are not the best fit. Just make sure that you communicate your denial in a way that is respectful. You also need to ensure that they know that you appreciated them taking the time to talk with you.

- Utilize multiple forms of communication. Instead of just telling them of your merits, show them. Bring photos, awards and other similar items that show them who you are and what you have accomplished.

Now, the majority of this chapter looked at selling yourself to an employer by using popular advertorial communication techniques. However, these work anytime you need to essentially show that you are the best or desirable. You can also use these techniques when you are dating, when you need assistance, or even when you are applying to college. These are all versatile and work for a number of situations. Just consider utilizing the right progression and making sure that all of your communication techniques are on point.

This is also a type of communication you can use during a debate or during a conversation when you want to best explain why your stance or opinions are what they are. It allows you to better connect with those listening to you and it makes it easier for you to be receptive to what they have to say.

Chapter 5: How to Read People Mastering Active Listening

Active listening describes the ability to get information from a group or a person. The active element of this communication technique means that you actively take certain steps to get information that is not automatically provided to you. Active listening is often combined with problem-solving and critical thinking because they are similar concerning their importance for effective communication. Remember that when it comes to communication, half the battle is hearing what the other person is saying and being able to understand it.

When you master active listening, it not only significantly improves your communication skills but also other elements of your life. Such benefits include:

- Boosts confidence

- Allows for easier development of mutual trust

- It results in you making fewer mistakes since it is easier to retain information

- Cooler heads will prevail

- You will be able to solve problems faster, resulting in increased productivity

- You will be able to avoid misunderstandings
- It allows you to build more meaningful relationships

Exploring the Techniques Associated with Active Listening

Active listening is so much more than just hearing what the other person has to say. It involves taking physical steps as the conversation evolves. The exact techniques to use will ultimately depend on your listening ability and the conversation. For example, if you are just chatting with a friend and catching up, you will generally use fewer techniques compared to when you are being briefed about an upcoming project at work. As you hone your active listening skills, it will become easier to determine which techniques are needed for which communication situations. The following are active listening techniques to work on:

- Building an atmosphere that is based on rapport and trust

- Showing that you understand by paraphrasing what the speaker is saying at the appropriate times

- Utilizing brief affirmations as you go about the conversation

- Seeking clarification by asking specific questions

- Showing your understanding of what they are talking about by disclosing similar experiences

- Demonstrating concern when this is appropriate

- Using the right nonverbal cues to show the person that you are engaged and listening

- Asking questions that are open-ended to encourage further discussion and to ensure that you fully understand the topic

- Not disclosing your opinions and thoughts until the time is appropriate

10 Steps to Becoming a Better Active Listener

When you are ready to start really honing your active listening skills, there are 10 steps that you want to start working through. Once you finish them, you will find that being a good, active listener is something that just now comes naturally to you:

1. When you are talking to someone, you want to maintain eye contact. Make sure that you are either sitting or standing in a way that allows the two of you to face each other.

2. You want to make sure that you are relaxed during the conversation – but be attentive. It is important that you

balance both of these because it can be off-putting if your listening appears to be too aggressive. This same step will have you work on filtering out any distractions. No matter where you are or how important a conversation is, distractions happen. If you allow them to capture your focus, the person speaking will notice and this can cause negative feelings.

3. Always make sure that your mind is open. Listen to their ideas, consider their perspective, take in any constructive criticism, and reserve judgment until you have heard everything that they need to say.

4. As the person is talking, make sure that you are hearing every word. As you are doing this, try to actually visualize what they are saying. In a nutshell, allow their words to essentially paint a picture for you.

5. Never force what you perceive to be the best solutions. It is also important that you do not interrupt the speaker. This can make the conversation hostile and cause the speaker to feel inferior or like they are not important to you.

6. Asking questions is a good thing, but you want to make sure that you do so at the right time. Give the speaker time to fully make their statement and

offer clarification before you ask for it. They may answer your questions before you even need to ask them.

7. When you are asking questions, ensure that they are meaningful and only to make sure that you understand the message they are trying to convey.

8. Try to put yourself in the speaker's shoes to feel what they are feeling as they speak.

9. Provide feedback as they are speaking. However, make sure that this feedback does not interrupt or distract them.

10. Look at all of the nonverbal cues that they are giving as they speak. This is often where you will see messages that are not spoken, but equally important.

Now that you have finished this chapter, it is easy to see why listening is so critical to effective communication. Active listening is a more advanced communication skill and it does take some time to hone. Now that you understand the different elements, the next step is to work on it, and before you know it, it will become natural for you.

Chapter 6: How to Read People Mastering Nonverbal Communication

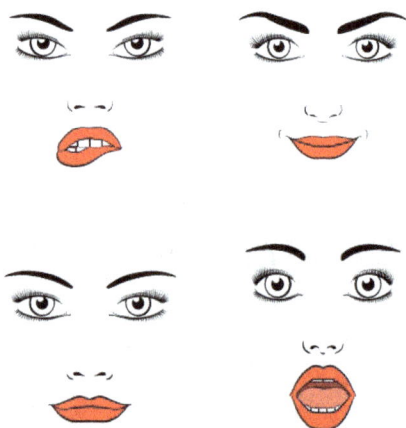

Nonverbal communication is divided into a number of different categories just like the verbal type. This type of communication is basically any type that is not verbal. Think about the body language used by the last person you spoke to. Did it match up with what they were saying? For example, you were worried about a friend and asked if they were okay and they said, "Yes." Did their body language also say "yes?"

Being able to control your body language and pick up on the nonverbal cues of others is critical to being able to communicate honestly and effectively. To put it simply, your body and your mouth need to match. If they do not, you are essentially sending mixed signals to the person you are talking with. Experts state that your nonverbal communication communicates your true feelings and desires. It is almost like a type of natural lie detector. In most cases, you do not realize that your body is not agreeing with your words. It is just natural and unconscious. However, when you learn advanced communication skills, you can better control it.

The way you look, react, listen, and move tells people more about what you are thinking than the words that you say. It also tells them if you are truly engaged in the conversation. People can also detect your level of truthfulness via your nonverbal signals. When your words and nonverbal cues do not match, this can create an atmosphere of mistrust, tension, and confusion.

The nonverbal cues that you exhibit during communication play several roles, including:

- Contradiction: This essentially means that your body language is telling a different story than your words.

- Complementing: This means that your body language complements your words. This can increase the overall emotion of the message that is being conveyed.

- Repetition: Body language may repeat the message that you are speaking.

- Substitution: This is when you use body language only to provide a message. For example, if someone rolls their eyes, this can convey annoyance without the person having to state that they are annoyed.

- Accenting: A verbal message may be underlined or accented by nonverbal communication. For example, if you are angry, as you are explaining the reason, you pound the table to accent this message.

Nonverbal Communication Types

There are different types of nonverbal communication that you want to get in tune with to ensure that you can better control them. It is important to not only know what these are but to have an understanding of what they encompass. Once you have this information, it makes it a bit easier to work on the nonverbal cues that you put out when you are communicating.

The first one to know about is facial expression. It is natural for the face to be very expressive. There are times every day where you use your face to display emotion. The one thing about facial expressions is that they are universal. This means that people tend to make the same face to display the same emotion. These expressions also tend to be the same across cultures. Your face can express:

- Happiness

- Anger

- Fear

- Sadness

- Surprise

- Annoyance

- Disgust

Your posture and body movements are the next elements to take a look at. How a person sits, stands, walks and holds their head tells the world how they are feeling. You often hear that some people carry themselves with confidence. This is because they utilize their posture and body language to communicate their confidence. Even the subtlest of movements or posture changes can give people important information about your mood and personality.

Eye contact is another major nonverbal cue. For most people, the visual sense is one that is best described as dominant. Being able to effectively use eye contact is critical to communicate in a way that is honest and genuine. How you are looking at someone when you are talking can communicate a number of things, such as affection, attraction, interest, and hostility. The flow of a conversation can be either interrupted or maintained by eye contact. Those you are talking to will examine your eye contact to determine if you are engaging in active listening and to see if you are truly interested in what they have to say.

Touch is another way to give people nonverbal cues. One good example is when you want to show someone that you are romantically interested in them. Psychologists state that touching a person's arm while talking can show them that you are interested without ever saying a word.

The following types of touch can tell people exactly how you are feeling:

- Handshakes

- Hugs

- Slap on the back

- Gripping the arm

- Shoulder tapping

- Pats on the head

Think about when you were a child and an adult patted you on the head and told you that you did a good job. This left you feeling happy, confident and reassured. Now, if their tone was sarcastic or cold when telling you "good job," you likely concluded that the pat on the head was more patronizing and not positive.

Space is something that you often study when exploring advanced communication. People who are close and having a warm conversation often do not have a lot of space between them. However, when there is hostility if you are talking to a person you do not know, there is likely more space between you. Personal space is important and when you let someone into your personal space, it indicates that you trust them and care about them. However, there are exceptions to this. For example, if you are arguing with a person and they quickly come into your personal space, this might signal aggression.

The tone of your voice is considered to be a form of both nonverbal and verbal communication. How you say something can be more important than the message you actually deliver. For example, if you are mad at someone and they ask if you are okay and you shout that you are, this tells them that you are not being honest. A person's tone can be used to deliver their true feelings.

There is no way to fake your nonverbal communication. You can control it better, but you can never fully use it to essentially fake out a person you are communicating with. Much of this type of communication is unconscious. This means that it just happens as you are communicating. If you try too hard to alter it, this will be obvious, and your overall communication will come across as dishonest and unnatural.

Improving Your Nonverbal Communication Skills

You need to put your full focus on working on your nonverbal communication. Just like you have to think before speaking, you need to also think before displaying nonverbal cues. One of the best ways to ensure that your nonverbal cues truly match your message is to get your stress under control. Yes, this is generally easier said than done, but it is not impossible.

When you are under a lot of stress, this can sometimes mask your nonverbal cues, making them come off wrong or differently.

You might also unconsciously exhibit off-putting cues that you do not even realize are happening. When you are under intense stress, it is best to take 30 minutes to yourself. Evaluate the situation and engage in some stress relief techniques. Try to avoid important conversation until you have a handle on your stress.

If you cannot avoid communication during times of intense stress, you should let those you are talking to know that you might not be yourself. This will let them know that your nonverbal cues might not be completely accurate.

Improve your emotional awareness to better your nonverbal communication. You must be able to recognize your emotions and their impact on you to send nonverbal clues that are accurate. Being able to determine the emotional state of others will also allow you to more accurately read their nonverbal cues. When you have a strong level of emotional awareness, you can:

- More accurately read the message others are conveying with their nonverbal communication and to determine if their words match their nonverbal cues

- Respond better so that the people you are talking to know that you care and that your care is genuine

- Create an atmosphere of trust in your relationships by making sure that your words and nonverbal cues match each other

- Determine if the relationships in your life best meet all of your emotional needs. This will make it easier to determine when to sever a relationship or when to foster it

Quick Tips to Help You Read Body Language

Once you are better at recognizing emotions and managing stress, you will naturally become much better at being able to read the nonverbal cues that other people put out. When you are reading these, consider the bigger picture. This means that you want to look at all of their nonverbal cues instead of putting your focus on just one. When you look at them all together, it gives you a much bigger picture of their true feelings.

Look for inconsistencies and do not dismiss them. Remember that verbal and nonverbal communication should match one another. If there are several times when they do not, this is something that should concern you.

Lastly, always trust your gut. If something is telling you that someone is not being honest with their words, believe it. By considering the inconsistencies, you will be able to easily tell if someone is being completely honest with you.

To sum it up, nonverbal communication is just as important as the verbal message you are trying to convey. When you are working to evaluate your own nonverbal cues, as well as those exhibited by others, pay attention to the following:

- Eye contact

- Tone of voice

- Touch

- Timing and place

- Facial expressions

- Gesture and posture

- Intensity

- Sounds

Conclusion

Thanks for making it through to the end of this book! Let's hope it was informative and able to provide you with all of the tools you need to achieve your goals whatever they may be.

The next step is to take your new knowledge and start applying it to your life. You can certainly see that with effective communication skills, it is much easier to find happiness and success in life.

Take one chapter and start working on it. For example, if you are looking to make a career change or you are seeking a promotion, start with the first chapter. While the basics of communication are the same in all areas, the more advanced techniques do differ. When you master your business communication, you are sure to find that your professional life is smoother. Then, choose the next area to work on.

As you work on your communication skills and mastering the advanced ones, you will start to notice a positive difference. Consider taking notes and treating this process as a regular learning opportunity. Track your progress and think about the areas that will benefit you the most.

Keep this book close while working on your communication. It includes all of the information that you need to be successful. This means that it will serve as a reference now and in the future when you want to sharpen your more advanced communication skills.

Improving your communication skills *really* doesn't have to be very difficult. It only needs the right strategies and determination to master effective communication.

Finally, if you found this book useful in any way, a review on Amazon is always appreciated!

CPSIA information can be obtained
at www.ICGtesting.com
Printed in the USA
BVHW092219080621
609009BV00010B/1467